Porcelain
Prompts Villains

Table of Contents

Writing Checklist:

1. Porcelain Prompts... Check!
2. Your Awesome Writing Skills... Check!
3. Throne to sit upon... we'll let you answer this one...
4. Porcelain Prompts pen/pencil...
5. Bookmark...

Don't have a Number 2 ready for your next prompt? We meant pencil. You can get a Porcelain Prompts bookmark, pen or pencil for free when you come see us at one of our appearances! Check the social medias (Facebook, Twitter, Instagram, YouTube) to find out where and when or check us out at SpinePressandPost.com

Now, Let's Get to Writing!

Prompt 1: Newfound Contempt

A villain often becomes a villain because they succumb to a temptation. The temptation for power, obsession, or greed. Write a story that involves temptation and the villain who fell to it.

_____

_____

_____

_____

_____

_____

_____

_____

_____

_____

_____

_____

_____

_____

Prompt 2: Despair Down

Many people turn to crime or villainy out of desperation. Write a story that begins with the moment of deep despair, then a choice that is made to make a character a villain.

_____

_____

_____

_____

_____

_____

_____

_____

_____

_____

_____

_____

_____

_____

Prompt 3: Casting a Shadow

Most villains are shadows of the hero. They both work toward the same goal, but their ways to achieve it are less moral. What is a goal that a hero and villain would both want to achieve?

_____

_____

_____

_____

_____

_____

_____

_____

_____

_____

_____

_____

_____

Prompt 4: Where There's a Will

What is your villain willing to do to achieve their goal that the hero is not?

_____

_____

_____

_____

_____

_____

_____

_____

_____

_____

_____

_____

_____

Prompt 5: An Alternate Route

What happened to your villain that prevented them from being able to take the heroic approach to achieving their goal?

_____

_____

_____

_____

_____

_____

_____

_____

_____

_____

_____

_____

_____

_____

_____

Crash Course: Antagonists vs. Villains

Thomas A. Fowler

What's the difference between an antagonist and a villain? It can sometimes be a fine line. But, when writing, it's key to understand the difference between an antagonist and a villain. Here's a key example: "Die Hard." The greatest anti-Christmas movie to ever exist and arguably the formula for tense action films. Hans Gruber is the villain. No doubt. He's the nefarious cause of all our troubles—as are his goons: the henchmen carrying out the plan and causing all these problems for John McClane. But, it's also got some great antagonists— people who cause problems for John throughout the narrative and make things harder for him to succeed.

You've got Chief Robinson, who is a well-intentioned high-ranking officer of the law. He means well, but doesn't respond well to McClane or Reginald VelJohnson's character's decisions. The Chief prefers to follow the book, he believes that's the way to end the conflict peacefully. He's not a bad guy, but he causes problems. That makes him an antagonist.

Then there are the FBI agents, both named Johnson. They are also antagonists because they are obsessed with glory and catching the bad guy. That obsession goes too far, and they cause problems upon their arrival. Nothing they do is necessarily terrible in intention, but the results often end horribly. That makes them antagonists.

Harry Ellis, Holly's coke-sniffing coworker, rides the line of antagonist and villain, but never crosses it. However, he's still never deliberately trying to harm anyone—and that's why he's not a villain. He just goes in thinking he can negotiate. He does coke, which is bad, but he doesn't force it on other people. Then, when everything goes to hell, he tries his best to talk John down and keep everyone safe. It's not great, he screws up big time, and we don't like him— but it doesn't make him a villain.

Then, you've got Richard Thornburg, the sleazy journalist trying to get dirt on the story over safety of the people in the building. Now, because he isn't part of the heist you could argue he's another antagonist. However, his actions are so deplorable I think he's actually a secondary villain. Here's why: all of the previous antagonists made horrible decisions, no doubt, but nothing they did was out of malicious intent. However, Thornburg is so obsessed with his populace and celebrity, he's willing to risk the safety of other human beings to get what he wants: ratings and attention on him. There's an argument that because he isn't with Gruber he's an antagonist, but the man reveals McClane's identity and essentially lets Gruber know his wife is in the building, thus setting up the finale. Any man who gave up my identity and compromised my family's safety is a straight up villain, whose comeuppance isn't nearly as brutal as it should have been.

Now this is just one example, but the reason it's such a good one is look at all the obstacles it sets up. I barely scratched the surface of Hans Gruber, who deserves books of analysis on why he's one of the greatest villains of all time. By inserting so many antagonists into the story, McClane has very few allies. It puts the stakes so highly against him that it seems he couldn't possibly ever succeed. It makes for great storytelling.

Prompt 6: Mundane Villainy

Some of the greatest villains are ordinary people in average situations. Find a seemingly mundane atmosphere and put the most interesting villain imaginable inside that atmosphere. How does their villainy play a part to foil the hero?

_____

_____

_____

_____

_____

_____

_____

_____

_____

_____

_____

_____

Prompt 7: Shifting Perspective

Many villains believe they are the hero of their own story. Write a backstory about a villain whose life led them to becoming a foil, yet in their eyes they are doing the right thing.

_____

_____

_____

_____

_____

_____

_____

_____

_____

_____

_____

_____

_____

Prompt 8: Heel Turn

Sometimes heroes switch sides. Write a story about a hero who loves the attention they get for defeating a crime. They start to commit crimes just so that they can receive the glory of saving the day.

_____

_____

_____

_____

_____

_____

_____

_____

_____

_____

_____

_____

_____

_____

Good vs. Evil: Why We Need Villains

Melissa Koons

Heroes are all the rage. What are they wearing? Who are they dating? What are their super powers? Who is their alter ego? Fans just can't get enough. If a hero is all that and then some, then why do we need villains?

Because the fictional world needs villains. Without a villain, who does the hero fight? Without a villain, what makes the hero a hero? Without the villain, what is the message/take away? Without a villain, what the heck is the story even about? Superman goes grocery shopping? Batman starts an emo rock band with Commissioner Gordon? Oooh, thrilling. What a page turner that would be.

Villains provide a dichotomy and a plot. More than that, villains provide perspective. Villains can show you a clear line of what is morally good, and what is morally evil. Villains can mirror real-life issues, and thus provide catharsis when they are defeated. Villains can make you look at the other side of the story and question what is really right, and what is really wrong. But the best villains are the ones that make you really consider those lines of good vs. evil.

We need villains because they make us think. They make us feel. They give the story purpose. Without them, what call to action would there be? Without them, what would be heroic? Without villains, what would be good?

Voldemort is a perfect example of the pure evil villain. He wants to destroy the humans and all "mudbloods" so that only the pure race of wizards remain. That's pretty awful, and any person who has taken a history class ever can tell you how that evil plan turns out (cough, WWII, cough.) Voldemort gives Harry and the wizarding community a cause. He clearly draws the lines of right and wrong and the moral obligation wizards have to protect those weaker than them (muggles.) Without Voldemort, the series would have been about a young boy learning he was a wizard and going to school. That still would have been entertaining, but what's the purpose? What's the meaning?

The real world is filled with horrible things and villainous people who hurt others. It is a constant battle that humanity has been fighting against since a group of them got together and decided to start civilization. A villain like Red Skull (Captain America's enemy,) gives a fictional face to embody these people and allows us to create a hero to fight against these very real problems. These real-life-turned-fiction villains allow us the opportunity to stand up and fight against injustice—and reach a cathartic end as they are ultimately defeated.

But, not everything in life is black and white. While Voldemort and Red Skull show clear lines of what is good and what is evil, other villains exist to make you question those lines. Some villains do it by providing motivation and backstory, like Magneto from *X-men*. He's faced persecution, imprisonment, torture, and all sorts of horrible things all because of what he is—something he has no control over. It's no wonder he wants to hurt those that hurt him and others like him. He thinks he is defending the mutants and protecting their existence—and in a way he is. But is it right? No… but I can see where he's coming from. Xavier wants to unite humans and mutants and have peace, Magneto wants to destroy humans and have peace. Same goal, but morally opposite paths to achieving it.

My favorite kind of villain, and the kind that I think has the most impact, is the type of villain that blurs that dichotomy of right vs. wrong, good vs. evil, and moral vs. immoral. These villains tend to be noble in nature and can really mess with your mind because you almost find yourself rooting for them to succeed. Unlike Magneto, who you know isn't going about it the right way and would really wish would stop fighting the X-men so that they could unite and actually get stuff done, these villains almost seem like heroes. A great example is Ozymandias from *Watchmen*. If you haven't read or seen *Watchmen*, then super spoilers ahead. Ozymandias is part of the Watchmen superheroes, but to protect the world from a nuclear war between the US and Russia (Cold War, anyone?) he takes matters into his own hands. He creates a massive monster and unleashes it on New York. He kills 2 million people, to save the world. With this new monster threat, the world forgets its squabbles and unites against a common enemy. Peace is achieved, but at a great cost. Was he right to do it? Was there another way? Was there a better way?

We need villains because they give significance and meaning to the actions. They make us think and evaluate morality. We need villains, without them we can't have a hero to save the day.

Prompt 9: The Crux Stops Here

Many villains are great because they seem unstoppable. Write about a character who appears to have no feasible way of being defeated. What is the one crux that can stop the villain?

_____

_____

_____

_____

_____

_____

_____

_____

_____

_____

_____

_____

Prompt 10: Gaining Mass

Villains amass followers, often by temptation. They allure loyalists to them by promising glory or power, something their followers desperately want. Write about a villain gathering a mass. Why are they gathering people? What do they promise to those loyal to them?

_____

_____

_____

_____

_____

_____

_____

_____

_____

_____

_____

_____

_____

Prompt 11: Crime and Reason

A good villain makes a good hero. What are 5 motivations a villain would have that would make readers want your hero to defeat them?

_____

_____

_____

_____

_____

_____

_____

_____

_____

_____

_____

_____

_____

_____

Prompt 12: Inner Workings

There are villains you love to hate, and therefore celebrate when they are finally stopped. Create a story around a villain that embodies the behavior or thing you hate the most.

_____

_____

_____

_____

_____

_____

_____

_____

_____

_____

_____

_____

_____

_____

Villains

52

Hip, Hip, Rue the day! Why we root For Villains

Thomas A. Fowler

Sometimes they're more interesting than the heroes. Sometimes they are too charismatic and you find yourself wooed by their charms. Sometimes villains are fighting for a cause they believe in. There are a number of reasons why we root for villains, but what's the larger reason why? How can we find ourselves inherently hoping someone making nefarious decisions succeeds? It makes for great storytelling, that's why.

One of the biggest storytelling notions is that the villain is only the villain because we're seeing the story from another perspective. If we were given the full story from the villain's perspective, we'd see that in their eyes they're not the bad guy. Rather, circumstances and horrendous situations made them who they are—oftentimes beyond their control.

In the novel *Red Dragon*, our hero, Will Graham, attempts to stop Francis Dolarhyde. Initially the killer seems like a true monster. However, as we get to know more about him, we realize he didn't become this serial killer all on his own. No, he was tortured, raised abusively by his grandmother and had no parents around to help him otherwise. As a result, this torture and abuse made him want to become something stronger, something greater: the Red Dragon. While we don't want him to succeed, per se, we also want him to get better. He shows indications of regaining his humanity, therefore he goes from a pure monster to a sympathetic villain. You see these hints and as he grows feelings for Reba McClane, you hope that she can show him the way to stop killing people. You cheer for him.

Another example of perspective for a villain is "Beasts of No Nation." In this case, our hero does some villainous things but because we see him go from an innocent boy stuck in a civil war to a child soldier, we cheer for him. As a result, we feel for him and understand why he's doing the things he's doing. We don't want him to do these horrible things, we want the innocent boy back. The same thing occurs with Idris Elba's character, Commandant. You hate who he's become, you despise the things he's doing and loathe that he's transforming children into soldiers. Yet, you know exactly why he's doing it and that motivation comes from a perspective of revenge because he found violence by the established government. So in his eyes, he's the hero. In reality he's not because of the deplorable acts of violence he takes among many other choices, but you understand where he's coming from, and that's a key for good villains: understanding their perspective.

It's rare you root for a villain who is evil just to be evil. Rare exceptions come in like The Joker, but that's because charisma takes over. The energy and performance of the character makes you like viewing the character. Again, you're not enjoying the fact that he's murdering people or sending a city into disarray. However, you get why they are the way they are, and their charisma makes their villainy enjoyable.

A recent case of everyone loving a villain is the Marvel Cinematic Universe's Loki. He's charming, and he's the slighted younger brother robbed of what he viewed as his rightful throne. Now, we've all felt cheated of things in life whether it be a promotion, or a big opportunity where they choose someone with better looks or because they know somebody. It happens to the best of us. As a result, we like Loki because he's lashing out against being wronged. We'd never do the disastrous things he does, but we get vicarious living for his ability to charismatically enact his revenge. We've all thought about sabotage, devious motivations, but we don't act out on them because we're decent human beings. By watching Loki, this chiseled-jawline, witty banterer trying to get what he deserves, we love him. We want to be him. People want to join his cause.

Those are some of the reasons why we love a good villain.

Prompt 13: Delectably Unlikeable

Villains can be captivating; someone you enjoy watching, despite knowing they're doing awful things. Take some alluring character traits and write a story that makes the main character a likable villain.

_____

_____

_____

_____

_____

_____

_____

_____

_____

_____

_____

_____

_____

Prompt 14: Ulterior Motive

What are 5 motivations your villain would have that you make you root for them to succeed?

_____

_____

_____

_____

_____

_____

_____

_____

_____

_____

_____

_____

_____

_____

Prompt 15: Loving the Hate

Who is your favorite fictional villain? Why do you love them? What would make you despise them instead? What's the line between the two?

_____

_____

_____

_____

_____

_____

_____

_____

_____

_____

_____

_____

_____

_____

_____

Prompt 16: A Dog Chasing Cars

Write a story: You have big plans for improving the chaos of the world—mainly by taking it over—but this pesky guy in tights keeps delaying your plan. How do you decide to defeat him?

_____

_____

_____

_____

_____

_____

_____

_____

_____

_____

_____

_____

_____

The Power of a Weak Villain

Melissa Koons

Villains are incredibly powerful characters. Not just because they want to take over the world or whatever, but because of the impact they have on your story and your plot. A great villain will challenge your hero. A great villain will give your hero a purpose. A great villain will make you understand why they are doing what they are doing and wish for their rehabilitation. A great villain will make you root for them—even when they are doing awful things. A great villain will make you question everything you know about good and evil.

But a weak villain will kill your story stone dead and ruin it.

You wouldn't think a single character, especially one that's not necessarily the main character or protagonist (some exclusions apply like Doctor Horrible— we're not talking about those stories, but it applies to them, too,) would have such a weighty impact on the quality of the story—but the villain does.

Why is that? What makes the villain so powerful to the plot that a weak character would make the world you built up come crashing down? Simple: if your readers can't understand the villain and their motivations, they won't understand your hero and their drive to stop them.

Have you ever read a book or watched a film where the villain was like one of those cardboard cutout villains from silent films with the handlebar mustache he can't stop stroking? It was kind of lame, right? You were sitting there wondering why on earth the hero was going to all this trouble over some weird guy with a strange allure to train tracks. If the villain holds no stake, then why does the hero care? Why do *you* care? Answer: you don't. That's why it all comes crashing down.

There are so many examples of weak villains who killed stories. Nick Cage's casting wasn't the only thing lame about 2007's "Ghost Rider." Did anyone else find the Devil's son, Blackheart, really anticlimactic? Or how about "Spiderman 3?" Just all of it. Venom was defeated by a bell. And later, by some musical pipe cage. (Yes, I watched it again so I could write this. I suffer for my art.)

Even Marvel isn't immune, one of the more anticlimactic villains was Justin Hammer from "Ironman 2." All he did was pay to get Mikey Rourke out of jail, the rest was super lame and why would this guy be an advisory to Tony Stark in or out of the suit? Why?

You can even take a great villain and ruin them by making their motivations weak, like Mr. Smith in "Matrix Revolutions." He was an incredible villain and personification of the machines in the first "Matrix" film, then he went and got all crazy and power hungry and suddenly humans and machines are calling a truce to take down this one dude who just keeps multiplying and this centuries old war is suddenly over (with a lot of Christ imagery.) Seriously? The One has to die for a computer virus? What, there's no Anti-Virus Malware Protection Software in the future? Just restore to the last back-up point and Mr. Smith will be wiped out and no one in the Matrix is the wiser. Come on, guys. I no longer have faith in our robot overlords.

M. Night Shyamalan has also received a lot of criticism for some of his films; most notably "The Village" and "The Happening." Both of these started off promising, but the villain fell WAY short. The villain in "The Village" ended up not being monsters, but people in costumes to protect the town from the horrors of the modern world. Interesting commentary, but lame villain. Similarly, "The Happening" ended up being plants releasing a chemical that made humans commit suicide. Great narrative about environmentalism, but a group of people running away from grass is pretty stupid.

I can go on and on about weak villains who ruined stories (Terminator Salvation, I don't even know who the villain really was other than Skynet doing something. I got so bored watching it my brain powered down and stopped paying attention.) I'm sure most of you have groaned and moaned while reading this article which dredged up so many unpleasant memories.

The point is, make a villain worthy of your hero. Give your villain a purpose and traits that gives your hero a challenge. A weak villain can ruin even the best of intentions.

Prompt 17: Mountain Out of a Molehill

Villains sometimes seem normal, but will surprise the hero later in the narrative. Write a story about someone who seems like an ally, but is revealed as the villain at the end of the story.

_____

_____

_____

_____

_____

_____

_____

_____

_____

_____

_____

_____

_____

_____

Prompt 18: Sidestep

Write a story: Tired of being a side character, a sidekick rises up and takes their revenge on the hero who prevented them from being the lead.

_____

_____

_____

_____

_____

_____

_____

_____

_____

_____

_____

_____

_____

_____

Prompt 19: Crowd-swerving

In most stories, the hero is able to defeat the villain. Write a story where the villain wins. What are the consequences? What are the benefits?

_____

_____

_____

_____

_____

_____

_____

_____

_____

_____

_____

_____

_____

Prompt 20: Adolescent Behavior

Write a story: A robber enters a bank and demands every last cent. What is their motivation? Does the villain get what they want? Are their actions glaringly villainous, or do we learn something unexpected that makes readers understand the villain's motivation?

_____

_____

_____

_____

_____

_____

_____

_____

_____

_____

_____

_____

_____

Meet the Creators

Thomas A. Fowler

At the age of 11, Thomas A. Fowler saw Jurassic Park. It was all nerdy as hell from there. Especially when he stuck around for the end credits and saw "Based on the novel by Michael Crichton." He went straight from the movie theater, walked down the mall to a Walden Books.

Since then, he's written movies, plays, short-stories and books. While he sticks primarily to science-fiction, he dabbles elsewhere. He holds an MBA in Marketing from Regis University and was a former Content Creator at a full-service ad agency in Denver, Colorado. Now, he devotes that skill set to a freelance career and to helping authors live their dream of getting published.

Somewhere, between writing and advertising, he tries to be a loving husband and responsible father.

Marketing Director at Spine Press & Post Publishing Services

Melissa Koons

Melissa Koons has always had a passion for books and creative writing. It may have started with Berenstain Bears By Stan and Jan Berenstain, but it didn't take long for authors like Lucy Culliford Babbit, Tolkien, and Robert Jordan to follow. From a young age she knew she wanted to share her love for stories with the world.

She has written and published one novel, multiple short stories, and poetry. She has a BA in English and Secondary Education from the University of Northern Colorado.

A former middle and high school English teacher, she now devotes her career to publishing, editing, writing, and tutoring hoping to inspire and help writers everywhere achieve their goals. When she's not working, she's taking care of her two turtles and catching up on the latest comic book franchise.

Publications Director at Spine Press and Post Publishing Services

GIVE YOUR BOOK THE BACKBONE IT DESERVES.

Spine Press + Post

COMPLETE PUBLISHING & MARKETING SERVICES
FOR AUTHORS & PUBLISHERS.

GET YOUR CUSTOMIZED SOLUTION AT
SPINEPRESSANDPOST.COM

WHO WOULD'VE THOUGHT LITERATURE & LATRINES MADE SUCH A GOOD PAIR?

KEEP THESE TWO TOGETHER

PORCELAINPROMPTS.COM

MORE PROMPTS ARE RELEASED ALL THE TIME!

Printed in Great Britain
by Amazon